Dr. Anastasia Tourta
Director of the Museum of Byzantine Culture in Thessaloniki

Eftychia Kourkoutidou-Nikolaïdou
Honorary Director of the Museum of Byzantine Culture in Thessaloniki

SHORT Guide

MUSEUM
OF BYZANTINE CULTURE

KAPON EDITIONS

The Museum of Byzantine Culture has been awarded
by the Council of Europe with the 'Museum Prize' for 2005.

Cover illustration: View of the Museum of Byzantine Culture.
Illustration on title page: Marble relief closure slab with griffins. 12th c.
Illustration on page 2: Detail of a wood-carved bema door. 17th c.

Fotographs: Makis Skiadaresis,
Museum of Byzantine Culture Archive
Translation: Dr. David Hardy
Proof Reading: Zeta Livieratou
Colour Separations: Stelios Anastasiou
Printing: E. Daniel Ltd S.A.
Binding: Eftaxiades - Iossiphides

© 2005 KAPON EDITIONS
23-27 Makriyanni Street, Athens 117 42, Tel./Fax: (210)9214 089, 9235 098
e-mail: kapon_ed@otenet.gr   www.kaponeditions.gr

ISBN: 960-7037-72-3

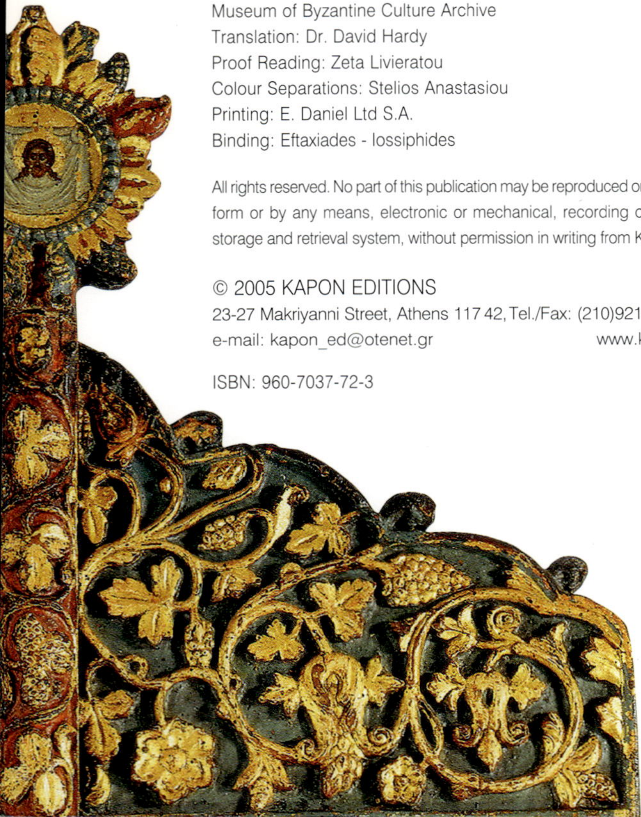

CONTENTS

INTRODUCTION

The purpose of the Museum of Byzantine Culture, as is suggested by its name, is to present the history, art and culture of the Byzantine world in Macedonia, particularly in Thessaloniki, the city that was the most important political, economic, intellectual and artistic centre in the European part of the Byzantine empire after Constantinople.

Byzantine culture, the successor to ancient Greek culture in the spheres of education and art, amalgamated and assimilated a variety of cultural elements. The transition from the ancient to the medieval world bore the decisive stamp of Christianity. The brilliance of Byzantine civilisation, which lived for more than a thousand years, crossed the borders of the empire in both East and West and captivated the peoples contemporary with it. The prestige and fame of Thessaloniki were particularly great in the Slav world and the general area of the Balkans.

The process of founding a Byzantine museum in Thessaloniki started in 1975, after the restoration of democracy in Greece. At the panhellenic architecture competition held in 1977, the first prize was won by the gifted architect Kyriakos Krokos, to whom is owed the spare, uncluttered building of the Museum of Byzantine Culture, a structure that has been considered the finest public building of our time and has been declared a protected historical monument and a work of art. The project was incorporated in the European Community's Integrated Mediterranean Programmes and was completed and handed over for use in October 1993. Since 1997, the Museum of Byzantine Culture has functioned as an independent provincial department of the Ministry of Culture. The Museum's museological programme envisages, in addition to exhibition rooms for the permanent display, a special wing for temporary thematic and temporary exhibitions, a special conference room – the 'Melina Mercouri' amphitheatre – for symposia and one-day scientific meetings, well-organised, functional antiquities storerooms, conservation laboratories, and a special room for educational programmes, enabling the Museum to function as a dynamic research and cultural centre.

The theoretical basis of the museological concept and method underlying the approach to the objectives of the Museum of Byzantine Culture was the desirability of creating a comprehensive communications channel with its public. Given this decisive parameter, the museum is not a display of artworks and artefacts from archaeological collections, but a display of ideas. The exhibits are not approached as works of art with an autonomous aesthetic and historical significance, but are selected and interpreted in such a way as to provide information on the historical, social, artistic or intellectual environment that produced them and to convert this information into knowledge – that is, a social asset. At a second level of reading, the background information accompanying the archaeological artefacts in the exhibition provides an academic and scientific interpretation of them, making it possible to reconstruct the human activities that created them. By thus integrating authentic objects into their historical context, modern museology approaches them as witnesses of the culture that produced them.

In this way, the Museum seeks to present as rounded a picture as possible of life in Byzantium, illuminating various aspects of its spirituality and art, social structure and religious life, and the daily life of its citizens in the countryside or in the major urban centres of the empire.

THE EARLY BYZANTINE PERIOD

(4TH – 7TH C.)

The first three rooms of the Museum are devoted to units relating to the Early Christian or Early Byzantine period, organised by subject. The beginning of this period is defined conventionally by the foundation of Constantinople in 325 and the transfer to it of the seat of the Eastern Roman empire. This period, a continuation of Late Antiquity which represented the end of the ancient world, saw the formation of the main features of Byzantine culture, bearing the decisive stamp of the new religion, Christianity. A unique synthesis of cultural features was accomplished within the space of the Eastern Roman empire, the main components of which were Greek language and education, Christianity as a spiritual and social force, Roman administration and Roman law, and eastern elements derived from the Hellenistic cities of the Mediterranean.

The Museum display deals with this long period of history in three thematic units, dealing with Early Christian churches as the main expression of the triumph of the Church, life in the towns and marketplaces and in the countryside as well as private life in the home, and finally Christian burials and burial customs, in which is reflected the Christian belief in the salvation of the soul and life after death.

Part of a ciborium from the church of Ayios Demetrios in Thessaloniki, on display in room 1. 5th-6th c.

Interior view of the church before the fire of 1917.

EARLY CHRISTIAN CHURCHES

After the recognition of Christianity as the official religion of the Eastern Roman empire by Theodosius the Great (379-408), large, opulent church complexes and churches were built, especially in the 5th and 6th century. Their size and numbers in the towns are often disproportionately large for the population, and they have therefore been seen as a means of projecting the triumph of the Christian Church over paganism, which now gives ground.

The predominant architectural type of Early Christian church is the basilica, which represents the adaptation of a Roman public assembly building to the liturgical practice of the Christian religion. The basilica is a long, narrow rectangular building divided by columns into three, five or seven aisles, to which is added the semicircular sanctuary apse at the east and the narthex at the west end of the church. A second type of Early Christian church consists of centralised buildings, whether circular, hexagonal or polygonal, which are found mainly in large martyria (churches built above the tombs of martyrs to the faith).

The Museum display devoted to Early Christian churches aims in presenting the church-building as a shell that serves the needs of worship and also promotes the aesthetic values of the day, as seen in the architectural sculptures of the church and its decoration and equipment with various objects and liturgical vessels.

The marble architectural sculptures of Early Christian churches consist of columns, column capitals and impost blocks of the long colonnades, closure slabs, sculpted lintels, and so on.

THE THEODOSIAN CAPITAL is the most characteristic type of Early Christian capital, and exhibits a new technique involving the pronounced use of the drill to render the hard, serrated acanthus leaves (fig. 1). The two-zone capital is a variation of the Theodosian capital, with serrated acanthus leaves on the basket, and with busts of

1   2

rams at the corners and doves in the middle of the sides. Another type is the tectonic capital, so-called from its shape. Stylisation is evident in the use of the drill to render the leaves (fig. 2).

Closure slabs are marble slabs placed in the spaces between columns to separate the side aisles from the central aisle, or between pillars to form a screen separating off the sanctuary.

CLOSURE SLAB CARVED ON BOTH SIDES, dating from the middle of the 6th century. Two endorsed birds are depicted at the centre of the slab, their heads turned towards the amphora between them. The main motif is surrounded by a maeander that encloses two running animals in the lower zone (fig. 3).

The mural decoration of Early Christian churches varies from the opulent churches of the capital and large urban centres to the less resplendent churches of smaller provincial towns. In opulent churches the walls were covered with costly wall mosaics, *opus sectile*, and marble revetment.

3 **DETACHED WALL MOSAICS** from the church of Ayios Demetrios depicting a peacock approaching to drink water from a bowl (fig. 4) and St Demetrios in supplication before the apse of a ciborium. To right and left are two figures of donors (fig. 5).

4

5

Floors were also covered with very expensive paving. In less wealthy churches, the floors consist of coloured mosaics, and the walls were covered with wall-paintings, a cheaper form of decoration.

6

DETACHED WALL-PAINTING from the Krypte Stoa in the Ancient Agora of Thessaloniki. In the upper zone can be seen an enthroned figure, and in the lower zone two bearded men in supplication, who have been identified with SS Kosmas and Damianos (fig. 6).

7

The equipment of Early Christian churches includes marble pulpits, which were used for reading from ecclesiastical books and for the sermon. There are three main types of Early Christian pulpit: a low pulpit reached by way of a staircase, a higher pulpit with two staircases set on its long axis, and the rarer **FAN-SHAPED PULPIT** with one entrance and two staircases (fig. 7).

RARE EXAMPLE OF A BOOK OF THE FOUR GOSPELS. The leaf on display in the Museum comes from the famous purple codex of the 6th century, which is known as the St Petersburg codex, since the larger part of it is now in this city. It is written in a majuscule script on parchment dyed purple. The letters of the text are silver, and the abbreviations IΣ (Jesus) ΘΣ (God) ΠHP (Father) are in gold letters (fig. 8).

8

9

SILVER RELIQUARY of the late 4th century in the shape of a rectangular casket. The four sides are adorned with symbolical representations in high relief of Christ Delivering the Law to the two leading disciples, Peter and Paul, of the Three Boys in the Fiery Furnace, of Daniel in the Lions Den and of Moses Receiving the Ten Commandments on Mount Sinai (fig. 9).

10

Another feature of the equipment of Early Christian churches consists of vessels used for lighting, such as copper-alloy lamps, *polykandela* (candelabra) and oil-lamps. **A BRONZE OIL-LAMP** of the 6th-7th century may be singled out (fig. 10). The suspension chains are still preserved and a glass vessel in which the wick burned, fuelled by oil, would have been placed in the hemispherical body. The inscription 'For the blessing of Patrikios and Eutropios' on the outside indicates that this is not simply a lighting vessel, but a dedication – an example of a pious offering.

EARLY CHRISTIAN CITY AND PRIVATE DWELLING

Another aspect of Byzantine culture parallel with intellectual and religious life consists of the everyday life of the citizens of the Byzantine empire, which rolled along with life's needs and problems, but also with the joys of family life. This aspect of culture is projected in the second room of the Museum. It is centred on the one hand on public life in the town and Agora, in professional workshops in the countryside and on the seas, and on the other on private life in aristocratic houses and in the homes of ordinary people. The Early Byzantine period is not marked by deep lines of cleavage in the organisation of public and private life like those caused by the advent of Christianity in intellectual and artistic output. The towns were still enclosed within walls, and the urban infrastructure, aqueducts and bathhouses, continued to be the same as they were in Late Antiquity. The centre of public life was the Agora, where various administrative services were located, along with public buildings such as theatres and the hippodrome. Next to the Agora there was usually the commercial market with shops and workshops processing raw materials.

11

MARBLE PEDESTAL of the 4th-5th century that probably supported a column or a statue. Three sides of the pedestal have niches with a seashell and a pediment crowning, in which are depicted relief full-length female figures wearing turreted crowns on their heads. These allegorical figures have been identified with personifications of towns and represent the Fortune of each. The one rendered as an Amazon with a shield has been identified with the Fortune of Rome, while the second, holding a cornucopia and fruit is thought to be the Fortune of Constantinople or Thessaloniki (fig. 11).

Aspects of daily domestic life include activities that took place in the house and also basic household chores, such as storing foodstuffs in vessels on the ground-floor of the house, preparing food with cooking vessels blackened by the smoke of the fire, with pestles, and with clay

and **GLASS TABLEWARE** (fig. 12). It also involved dressing the family, that is, spinning the wool, weaving on the loom, sewing the clothes, as well as care for personal appearance, with cosmetics and jewellery. At the centre of the display is a **TRICLINIUM**, that is, an apsidal reception room, of an urban house in 5th-century Thessaloniki. The rectangular room has a mosaic floor, with geometric and floral motifs. A panel of the mosaic contains an inscription praying for happiness for the members of the owners' family. At the west end of the triclinium room is a semicircular apse, one step higher than the rest, on which the couches were placed. The walls of the room are covered with paintings in rectangular frames imitating marble revetment (fig. 13).

The **CHITONS** on display are on loan from the Benaki Museum. They come from tombs in Egypt where they were preserved by the lack of humidity in the sandy soil. One chiton, dating from the 5th century, is of undyed linen with a woollen decorative weave in a brown-red colour (fig. 14). The other chiton, dating from the 7th century, is woollen, dyed red, with decorative circular attachments sewn to it (fig. 15).

15

14

14

FROM THE ELYSIAN FIELDS
TO THE CHRISTIAN PARADISE

Organised as part
of the European
Science Foundation
research project
'The Transformation
of the Roman World,
AD 400-900', with
the support of the
European Union,
RAPHAEL
Programme.

The Elysian Fields of the ancient Greeks were a paradise of material well-being and enjoyment for the chosen of the gods. In contrast, the Christian Paradise is a heavenly place that symbolises the salvation of the souls of believers and life after death. This substantial difference in the Christian world-view is given distinct expression in the iconography of tombs, in the symbols and the texts of funerary inscriptions, and also in burial customs, existing alongside survivals from the ancient world. In ancient times, the cemeteries extended outside the fortification walls of towns. From the 2nd to the 3rd century, Christian burials took place in the same areas, in the existing 'pagan' cemeteries. Gradually, special Christian cemeteries were organised around the tombs of martyrs, and then in areas organised by the local Church.

Many of the graves had markers that consisted of marble or stone slabs bearing Christian symbols such as the cross, the chi-rho monogram, the fish, doves, and/or inscriptions containing expressions that indicate the new relationship of the Christian with death: it was a fundamental belief that the grave was a place where the deceased slept until the Last Judgement and the resurrection of the dead. These expressions include 'sleeping place until the resurrection', 'sleeping well', 'I enjoy eternal life', 'in memory' etc.

There is a particularly rich collection of wall-paintings from the Christian tombs in Thessaloniki dating from the 3rd to the 6th century. The subjects handled by funerary painting come either from the Old and New Testament and have an eschatological content, or contain symbols and allegories relating to doctrines of the new religion, such as life after death and the salvation of the soul. Symbolic subjects of this kind include the lamb, the dove, the deer approaching to drink water, peacocks flanking kantharoi, etc.

THE TOMB OF SUSANNAH. The painting of a 5th-century

16

tomb narrates the allegorical story of Susannah in the Old Testament (fig. 16). Susannah is depicted in a garden with trees and fences, her hands raised in a stance of supplication, between two old Jewish men who have unjustly accused her of adultery. Susannah prayed to God and was vindicated.

The story of Susannah is an allegory of the triumph of the Church of Christ over the heretics.

TWIN VAULTED TOMB of the 4th century. One of the tombs is covered with painting imitating coloured marble revetment. On the east narrow end of it is depicted a bird with spread wings in a plane of flowers, while the west narrow end has a wreath between two doves, enclosing a chi-rho monogram. On the ceiling vault are wreaths with leaves (fig. 17). The second tomb is decorated with scenes from the Old and New Testament, which share a common feature in their allegorical reference to the Lord's work of redemption. These scenes include Moses

17

18

and the burning bush, the tablets with the Ten Commandments, Daniel in the Lions' Den, the Good Shepherd, the Raising of Lazarus, Adam and Eve next to the tree with the snake, and so on (fig. 18).

THE TOMB OF EUSTORGIOS of the 4th century. The decoration of this tomb includes a rare representation of a family performing the funeral customs in honour of their dead forefathers. The family consists of Flavius, Aurelia, their two children and the aged 'mother of all', standing around a funerary altar on which sits a libation vase (fig. 19).

Finds inside tombs are also very important, in that they provide information on burial practices and also on the social and economic conditions of the period. Bronze coins inside and outside the tombs, gold *danakai*, which were placed instead of a coin on the mouth of the dead, following the ancient custom, vases and ceramic vessels for funeral banquets and libations of liquid offerings during interments, glass and clay funerary vases, and **JEWELLERY AND DECORATIVE ATTACHMENTS** (fig. 20) from the clothing of the deceased – all these form a moving reference to the people of that period and their feelings towards their dead.

20

FROM ICONOCLASM TO THE SPLENDOUR OF THE MACEDONIAN AND KOMNENIAN DYNASTIES (8TH – 12TH C.)

The religious and ideological crisis of the iconoclastic controversy that shook the Byzantine empire in the 8th and 9th century also had political and social repercussions. At the same time as persecuting the icons, the iconoclastic emperors attempted to implement measures against ecclesiastical and monastic property, since the monks were the main representatives of icon-worship. After the end of the crisis, monasticism recovered and many large monasteries and monastic centres were founded, Mount Athos amongst them. At the same time, the imperial policy regarding the Slav world led to a proselytising mission to the Slavs of central and eastern Europe, led by the brothers Cyril and Methodios from Thessaloniki, to whom is owed, besides the spread of Christianity, the creation of the first Glagolitic Slavonic alphabet.

The contraction of the east and west borders of the empire at this period resulted in greater homogeneity within it. Castle-cities were founded on naturally strong sites to counter hostile raids.

The iconoclastic policy also had repercussions on the decoration of churches, which were dominated by aniconic, geometric, floral and zoomorphic motifs, with particular prominence given to the symbol of the cross. After the end of the iconoclastic controversy in 843, new iconographic programmes were developed in church wall-painting, with the symbolical position occupied in the church by each representation being fixed in an order that reflected the heavenly hierarchy. A new architectural type also gradually evolved in church-building: the domed cross-in-square church, alongside which simple and composite octagonal churches also became predominant, particularly in the *katholika* of large monasteries. Particular attention was paid to the decoration of the facades with cloisonné masonry and the use of decorative brickwork.

A distinctive feature of this period are large relief icons of saints carved in marble. The **RELIEF ICON OF THE VIRGIN ORANS** dates from the early 11th century. The Virgin is depicted standing and in supplication. Her head is missing. The drapery of the garments is soft, allowing the volume of the body to show through (fig. 21).

Already in the Early Christian period sacred places of pilgrimage had developed, mainly in the Holy Land, where Christ lived his earthly life, and also at the tombs

of apostles, saints or martyrs. In Thessaloniki, the churches of the myrrh-emanating SS Demetrios and Theodora were centres of veneration. Emperors and illustrious officials were presented with *lythron* (earth mixed with blood from the tomb of St Demetrios) in reliquaries that took the form of models of his tomb. From the middle of the 12th century onwards, pilgrims took from the tombs of these saints myrrh contained in **LEAD VIALS**, known as *koutrouvia* (fig. 22).

22

A new feature of this period is the legitimising of the interment of the dead inside the city, in the courtyards of churches and monasteries. The graves are usually simple pits bounded by stones and bricks, and containing the personal items of the dead person, particularly jew-

23 ellery. At the same time, there are more complex funerary structures, pseudo-sarcophagi and arcosolia, inside the churches, in which eminent clerics or laymen were buried. The **SLAB OF A PSEUDO-SARCOPHAGUS** dating from the 10th century is decorated with interlaced motifs and palmettes (fig. 23).

The manuscript of an 11th-century **LECTIONARY** on display is a work of fine art. Written on thin parchment, it contains passages from the four gospels that are read in church on Sundays. It is adorned with miniatures of the four evangelists, of which only three – Matthew, Mark and Luke – are now preserved. The evangelists are depicted sitting in front of lecterns, with the equipment needed for writing. The headpieces bordering the titles of the text, and the initial capitals of each chapter, are of particular

24b

24a

24c

interest from the point of view of decoration. The dimensions, the fine script and the rich decoration assign the Lectionary to a scriptorium in Constantinople (fig. 24a-c).

THE ICON OF THE VIRGIN DEXIOKRATOUSA dates from about 1200. The Virgin is depicted holding Christ on her right arm, and holding out her left hand towards her Child. Her face has delicate, aristocratic features and a sorrowful expression. In contrast, the face of Christ, who rests a scroll on his thigh, is fleshy and has strong fea-

25

26

27

tures. Probably a work imported from Cyprus (fig. 25).

A new feature of this period is connected with ceramic technology: the glazing of domestic pottery, especially tableware. A layer of glaze on the surface of these pots made them waterproof. Glazed pottery has painted, sgrafitto or relief decoration (figs. 26, 27).

THE GOLD BRACELETS on display, dating from the 10th century, are luxury goods – dress accessories worn by aristocratic Byzantine ladies. They are made in the difficult cloisonné enamel technique. The motifs on them are birds pecking at grapes, palmettes, and rosettes (fig. 28).

28

THE DYNASTIES OF BYZANTINE EMPERORS

From the time of the emperor Heraclius in the 7th century onwards, a significant change may be observed in the succession to the throne, with the monarchy becoming hereditary. The emperors usually crowned their successor as co-ruler during their lifetime. This secured hereditary succession within the family, which in turn led to the great imperial dynasties.

The table of the Byzantine dynasties on display has depictions of emperors in mosaics, manuscript miniatures, works of minor art and coins. These furnish evidence for the royal dress, in purple, and the crown, the symbol of imperial authority. Other emblems of authority held by the emperor included a globe with a cross, symbolising the Ecumene and the predominance of Christianity within it, and the sceptre or a purple purse containing earth, which symbolised the mortality of kings. The main vehicle of the dissemination of imperial policy and ideology consisted of coins with the figure of the emperor, which were widely circulated and indicated that royal authority stemmed from God.

THE GOLD SOLIDUS issued by the mint of Thessaloniki has a depiction of the emperor Honorius (393-410) on one side and on the other the personification of Constantinople enthroned, holding a sceptre and being crowned by Victory (fig. 29a-b).

29a   29b

Coins bore a depiction of the emperor on one side and Christ blessing on the other. Coins struck at the mint of Thessaloniki had, in addition to depictions of Christ and the Virgin, a representation of St Demetrios, the patron saint of the city.

From the 11th century onwards the gold solidus, the main monetary unit of Byzantium since the time of Constantine the Great, was replaced by a new gold coin, the hyperpyron, as part of the economic policy of Alexios I Komninos designed to counter the acute economic crisis faced by the state.

30

A new element in Byzantine coinage of the Middle Byzantine period are the so-called *skyphota* coins, which were convex and concave.

The display also contains hoards of coins which were set aside as savings or concealed in times of war. Amongst them we may note the hoard of coins issued by the emperors Basil II (976-1025), Romanos III (1028-1034) and Constantine IX (1042-1055) (fig. 30).

BYZANTINE CASTLES

The theme of this display is Byzantine castles, the construction of which during the Middle Byzantine period (9th-12th c.) was the outcome of a series of historical and political junctures during the preceding centuries. Enemy raids, economic difficulties, and natural disasters such as major earthquakes and epidemics of plague, all contributed to the gradual contraction or even abandonment of the large Early Christian towns. The stable conditions that prevailed in the empire from the 9th century on were also manifested in intense building activity, with repairs to existing fortresses and the construction of new castles.

Castles controlled passes, protected the productive land, and served the needs of defence and residence. On them were concentrated the basic functions of a town, though it was the morphology of the terrain and the limited space in which they were built that determined their urban design and the architecture of the houses. The 6th, 9th, 10th and 14th centuries saw the greatest activity in the construction of fortification works. A dense network of castles was erected between Constantinople and Thessaloniki, many of them built along the Via Egnatia.

31

The exhibition makes use of archaeological material and audio-visual aids to present the reasons and preconditions for the creation of Byzantine castles, their urban design, the crucial question of securing a water-supply so that they could offer effective defence, the organisation of life within the castle, the relationship between the castles and the countryside, since rural society played a decisive role in Byzantium, and finally, siege tactics and military equipment. The archaeological material on display comes from various castles in Macedonia, particularly the one at Rendina, 71 km north-east of Thessaloniki, which was systematically excavated by Professor N. Moutsopoulos. The exhibition is supplemented by a video produced by the painter Marianna Strapatsaki, presenting the castles of north Greece, from the westernmost castle of Angelokastro on Corfu to the easternmost, Pythio, in Thrace.

THE FORTIFIED BYZANTINE SETTLEMENT OF RENDINA

32

was built on the summit of a hill that controlled the route from central to eastern Macedonia and Thrace. It was successor to the fortress of Artemision built in the 6th century, which was in turn built on the site of an existing Roman fort (fig. 31). From the 9th century onwards it is referred to as the headquarters of the See of Lete and Rendina. Inside the castle still stands a **CHURCH WITH A**

33

CRUCIFORM GROUND-PLAN (fig. 32) and a Middle Byzantine basilica, and excavations have also revealed workshops, houses, a large number of cisterns to collect rainwater, and cemeteries. There is also an impressive staircase dug into the ground, leading from the castle to a large cistern next to the stream at the foot of the hill, which supplied the castle with water.

During the excavation of the tower on the citadel of Gynaikokastro in the prefecture of Kilkis, **PART OF A WALL-PAINTING** came to light, bearing the monogram of the Palaiologan dynasty. This monogram provides confirmation for the historical sources, which state that the castle in question was built by Andronikos III Palaiologos (1328-1341), and also attests to the existence of a chapel with wall-paintings on one storey of the tower (fig. 33).

ROOM 7

THE TWILIGHT OF BYZANTIUM, 1204-1453

The organisation of the exhibition and the conservation of the exhibits were sponsored by

Groupe **Carrefour**

CARREFOUR MARINOPOULOS S.A.

"In memory of Ioannis P. Marinopoulos".

This exhibition unit deals with the last centuries of the life of the Byzantine empire, a critical period of history bounded by two captures of Constantinople: the first in 1204 by the Latins of the Fourth Crusade, the second and final in 1453 by the Ottoman Turks, which signalled the end of the empire after about eleven centuries of life. During this period, despite the adverse circum-

34b

34a

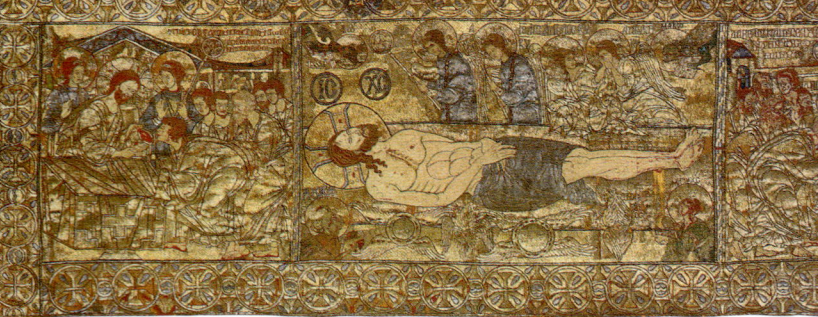

stances created by the continual contraction of the territory of the empire, particularly in the light of the advance of the Ottoman Turks, economic recession and civil wars, the arts and letters experienced a fresh flowering, centred mainly on Constantinople and Thessaloniki.

As long as the Latins held Constantinople (1204-1261), the centre of art shifted to Thessaloniki. The city, liberated from Latin rule as early as 1224, gave form to the new trends and disseminated them both to Greek areas and to the territories of the Serb rulers. Even after the recapture of Constantinople by Michael VIII in 1261 and the reestablishment of the Palaiologan dynasty, Thessaloniki retained its role as an artistic centre on equal terms with the capital, though with different aesthetic aspirations. Its reputation and influence extended to Mount Athos and the neighbouring Slav peoples.

34c-d

Representative artworks of this period are presented in the exhibition, incorporated into the historical background just described.

THE 'THESSALONIKI EPITAPHIOS', a masterpiece of ecclesiastical gold-embroidery dating from about 1300, forms the centre-piece of the display.

The dead Christ is depicted at the centre of the epitaphios, surrounded by hosts of angels. At the edges are depictions of the Communion of wine and the Communion of bread administered by Christ to the Apostles. The composition and monumental style of the representations links the embroidery with works of large-scale painting from the beginning of the 14th century, while the technical excellence of its manufacture makes it an outstanding work of ecclesiastical embroidery of its time (fig. 34a-d).

Around the epitaphios are placed a number of items of great doctrinal and aesthetic importance, such as the famous icon of Christ as the 'Wisdom of God', the precious icon of the Virgin and Child, other icons, two of which are painted on both sides, and detached wall-paintings; all these are works from Thessaloniki that attest to the excellent level attained by art in the city during the 14th century.

In the **ICON OF CHRIST AS 'THE WISDOM OF GOD'**, the monumental figure of Christ, with his intense facial features, is animated by an expressionist, anticlassical spirit characteristic of works of the 14th century, particularly the second half of it. The appellation of Christ as 'Wisdom of God', and the monumental dimensions of the icon suggest that it came from the templon of the church of Ayia Sophia in Thessaloniki (fig. 35).

THE ICON OF THE VIRGIN AND CHILD, with its balanced composition, tranquil ethos and the painterly modelling with soft chiaroscuro, is an outstanding example of painting in Thessaloniki during the early 14th century (fig. 36).

THE DETACHED WALL-PAINTING from the katholikon of the Vlatadon Monastery in Thessaloniki, depicts a fragment of Pentecost. It dates from between the years 1360 and 1380 and, together with other wall-painting ensembles preserved in churches in the city, reveals the high level attained by painting in the second half of the 14th century (fig. 37).

The continued tradition of marble relief icons is attested by the two items on display here, while bas-relief sculp-

35

36

37

38

tures using coloured
ceromastich in the back-
ground were a characteristic feature of the period.

THE OMPHALION, A CIRCULAR SCULPTURE of the 13th
century depicts an eagle tearing apart a hare in a vine-
yard. The omphalion adorned the floor of the church of
Ayia Sophia at Trebizond in Pontos, founded by the emperor Manuel X Komninos (1238-1263). It was brought to
Thessaloniki in 1924 by refugees from Pontos (fig. 38).

The **RELIEF MARBLE ICON** of the 13th-14th century depicts Hosios David of Thessaloniki in supplication and
wearing a monk's habit. The saint withdrew to a mon-

39

astery outside the city in the 6th century. Marble icons were costly items and workshops manufacturing them were to be found only in the large cities of the empire, such as Constantinople and Thessaloniki (fig. 39).

A series of works of a funerary nature, such as inscribed grave stelai, grave offerings, relief slabs for pseudo-sarcophagi, the rare monolithic sarcophagus of Theodoros Kerameus, archbishop of Ohrid, and the fragment of a funerary monument found in the church of Ayia Sophia in Thessaloniki, all provide a wide range of information on the burial practices, painting, sculpture and prosopography of the period. The mint of Thessaloniki, which is characterised by lavish, original numismatic types, is also presented.

The display of a large number of **GLASS VASES** not only confirms the flowering of glasswork in the city, but also, through the imported items, attests to commercial contact with Venice and the Islamic East (figs. 40-42). Visual

40

41

aids deal with the cultural life of Thessaloniki, which was manifested above all in a revival of interest in ancient literature and the cultivation of Classical and Law studies, a sphere in which Thessaloniki can claim two great figures in Konstantinos Armenopoulos and Matthaios Vlastaris. Attention is also drawn to the importance of the city to the empire, which is also attested by the frequent and/or long-term residence in it of the emperor and members of the imperial family.

This exhibition unit is completed by the presentation on the mezzanine floor in this room of the pottery workshops identified in Macedonia and Thrace. Taking technological issues and innovations in pottery production as the starting point, the products of the **POTTERY WORKSHOPS OF THESSALONIKI** (fig. 43), Serres and Mikro Pisto in the Rodopi Mountains are presented, along with the extent of their commercial spread.

42

43

THE DORI PAPASTRATOU COLLECTION

In 1993, the daughters of Dori Papastratou donated the collector's large, unusually varied, collection of Greek religious engravings to the Museum. Of the 198 engravings contained in the Collection, dating from the 18th to the early 20th century, 29 selected pieces are displayed in this room.

Orthodox religious engravings are a visual genre with origins in the West. The genre first appeared in the late 14th century, and the historical juncture obliged the Orthodox Church, particularly the large monasteries, to adopt it about the middle of the 17th century. The Sinai

44

Monastery was the first to use engravings, on a wide scale, as a means of self-promotion and communication with the faithful. **THE TINTED WOODCUT** depicts St John of the Ladder, a hermit who withdrew to the Sinai desert and later became abbot of the Sinai Monastery. The engraving was printed in 1700 at Leopolis (Lviv), formerly in Poland and now in the Ukraine, and was commissioned by the monastery (fig. 44).

The engravings, which depicted panoramic views of

45b-c

monasteries and a large number of vivid details, were the main means of communication between the monasteries and the scattered Orthodox congregation, to whom they were distributed as 'blessings', in an exhortation to them to provide financial support. The **KYKKOS MONASTERY** on Cyprus, for example commissioned an engraving printed in Venice in 1778. It depicts the monastery, the miraculous icon of the Virgin painted, according to tradition, by St Luke the evangelist and commissioned by the Virgin herself, and the miracles worked by the icon (fig. 45a-c).

THE ENGRAVING OF THE MONASTERY OF ST PAUL ON MOUNT ATHOS depicts the fortress complex of the monastery, with the surrounding area and the ancillary buildings. The representations in the upper part of the engraving and the inscriptions accompanying them give prominence to the sacred heirlooms owned by the monastery. The engraving was printed in Vienna in 1798 (fig. 46a-c).

Engravings depicting holy figures (Christ, the Virgin, saints) had the same value as objects of veneration for the faithful as painted icons, which they replaced on the icon-stands in the houses of the economically weaker classes. At first, the Orthodox engravings were printed in European cities that had both the required technology and strong Greek communities, for the cost of printing the engravings was usually shouldered by Greek merchants of the diaspora. Later, however, engraving workshops were founded on Mount Athos, which met the needs of the entire Orthodox world.

The items shown in the exhibition represent all the main places in which Greek engravings were printed: Leopolis (Lviv) in the Ukraine, Venice, Vienna, Constantinople and Mount Athos. Some of the engravings on display are very valuable, in that they are the only surviving copies.

46b-c

46a

THE DIMITRIOS EKONOMOPOULOS COLLECTION

The Dimitrios Ekonomopoulos Collection was presented to the Museum in 1987 by his widow Anastasia Zamidou-Ekonomopoulou, in accordance with the provisions of his will. The Collection was placed on display on two storeys of the White Tower for a few years, before finding its final place in the Museum. It consists of material from a variety of genres and periods, in which icons are predominant in terms both of numbers and quality. The Museum acquired 1,460 items, of which only a selection is on display.

Representative items of every category were selected for the exhibition, in order to give visitors an idea of the broad spectrum of the collector's interests and aspirations. They include: pottery, mainly Byzantine and Post-Byzantine glazed tableware dating from the 12th to the 16th century, and a number of earlier items from the 5th-

47

48

7th centuries, such as the clay pilgrim flask from the shrine of St Menas in Egypt. Of the 630 coins in the Collection, covering a period of about 1,600 years, 96 are on display, dating from the 1st c. BC to the 17th c. AD. Also displayed are a number of metal artefacts, most of them ecclesiastical, dating from the 6th to the 19th century, a document of Kallinikos IV, Patriarch of Constantinople (1801-1806, 1801-1809) and above all, icons, which form the main bulk of the Collection.

The icons represent almost all the painting schools and trends that evolved from the end of the 14th to the 19th century, offering a panorama of Orthodox art. Those on display are grouped either by kind, such as icons for private worship, templon icons, etc., or by iconographic themes. Thanks to this latter arrangement, attentive visitors have an opportunity to see the various iconographic treatments given to a subject, to follow its development over time, and to appreciate how it was conceived and rendered by various schools of painting.

THE ICON OF ST ATHANASIOS OF ALEXANDRIA, dating from the 15th century and one of the earliest in the Ekonomopoulos Collection, is a notable work of the Cretan School (fig. 47).

THE EARLY 16th CENTURY ICON with a representation of the Adoration of the Magi is a characteristic example of Italian-Cretan art, and demonstrates the Cretan painters' ability to produce works to suit the taste of both Orthodox and Catholic clients (fig. 49).

49

THE ICON OF CHRIST PANTOKRATOR, with Greek and Slavonic inscriptions, was commissioned by the Serb archbishop Paisios of Peć (1640-1641) in a Greek workshop, probably on Mount Athos (fig. 48).

'BYZANTIUM AFTER BYZANTIUM'

THE BYZANTINE LEGACY AFTER THE FALL OF CONSTANTINOPLE (1453-19TH C.)

The organisation was partly funded by the European Union, Operacional programme CULTURE, CSF III.

The display is devoted to elements of the art and culture of Byzantium that survived in the Greek world after the capture of Constantinople by the Ottoman Turks in 1453.

Post-Byzantine art, which was primarily religious art, developed under new conditions that were directly related to the nature of the rule to which the Greeks were subjected. In the 15th century, the favourable conditions that prevailed in the Greek regions under Venetian rule, and the fertile contacts with the West, led to the creation in Crete of a school of painting which was based on earlier Palaiologan art and creatively assimilated elements of contemporary and earlier Italian painting. After the capture of Crete by the Ottomans in 1669, the artists and paintings that migrated to the Ionian islands contributed to the creation of the so-called Ionian School, which was to some extent the successor to the Cretan School. By contrast, in the regions under Ottoman rule, subjugation to a conqueror of a different faith encouraged adherence to more conservative versions of Byzantine art, with very few exceptions.

In the 16th century, the large monastery centres in Greece, particularly those on Mount Athos, became the main vehicles of the advancement of art; they assigned large-scale projects both to Cretan painters and to painters of the school that evolved in north-west Greece in this century. Mount Athos also retained its role of regulator in maters of art in the 18th century, when a painting movement of a learned character developed there, with trends that harked back to early 14th century painting in Macedonia.

Against this general background, the exhibition presents, on two opposite sides of the room, works representative of the trends and painting schools over time in the areas of Greece ruled by the Ottoman Turks and the Venetians. On the **TWO BOARDS FROM A TEMPLON EPISTYLE**, the apostles are depicted from the waist up, beneath a relief arch, with various stances and gestures. The epistyle is attributed to the fine painter Frangos Katelanos, the supreme representative of the North-West Greek School of the 16th century (fig. 50).

50

THE ICON OF THE VIRGIN GALAKTOTROPHOUSA was executed in 1784 by the painter Makarios from the village of Galatista in Chalkidiki. Makarios and his team are known mainly from wall-paintings executed by them in monasteries on Mount Athos (fig. 51).

51

THE ICON WITH THE JUDGEMENT OF POTIPHAR and the other three on display form part of a broader group of icons now dispersed in various European museums and collections. They depict the story of Joseph from the Old Testament, and were painted between 1677 and 1682

52

by the Cretan painter Theodoros Poulakis, who in several cases used Flemish copperplate engravings as his models (fig. 52).

The display also deals with some individual themes that made their appearance for the first time in the Post-Byzantine period. One is the emergence of religious engravings, a new genre of visual expression adopted by the Orthodox Church from the West in the 17th century. The second theme is the neomartyrs, the veneration of whom was promoted by the Orthodox Church in order to strengthen the morale of the sorely tried Christians through their example, and check the wave of conversions to Islam. In the latter case, the engravings contributed to the spread of the veneration of the neomartyrs they depicted.

53

THE ENGRAVING, which dates from the middle of the 19th century, depicts the neomartyr Georgios of Ioannina, wearing the characteristic local costume. The saint was martyred in 1838 and sanctified by the Orthodox Church very soon after his death (fig. 53).

Another theme touched upon is the flowering of monasticism in the 16th century in Macedonia outside Mount Athos, through the presentation of icons depicting leading personalities of monasticism, such as St Dionyssios of Olympos and St Nikanor of Zavorda, who contributed to its spread.

THE ICON OF 1788 DEPICTS HOSIOS NIKANOR holding a model of the Zavorda Monastery founded by him. The saint was highly active in West Macedonia and is one of the most important figures of 16th-century monasticism (fig. 54).

54

A few excellent examples of ecclesiastical gold-embroidery are also exhibited, including the **GOLD AND SILK SAKKOS**, which belonged to Bishop Ioannikios of Melenico (1745-1753). The inscription embroidered on the heavy material states that it was made by Christophoros Zefarovitch, a talented artist who executed wall-paintings and icons, engravings and ecclesiastical gold-embroideries (fig. 56a-b).

THE PEARL-STUDDED GOLD AND SILK EPIMANIKIO has a rare subject. It was made for Gerasimos from Crete, Bishop of Thessaloniki (1788-1810), who is depicted kneeling before St Demetrios, with the walled city in the background (fig. 55).

Finally, there is a display of liturgical books and splendid examples of ecclesiastical silverware. Most of the latter are on loan from the Benaki Museum.

In the corridor outside the entrance to the main room are two showcases, one devoted to elements of private life and the other to products of glazed-pottery workshops, which continued to use the manufacturing technology and decorative techniques of the previous Byzantine period.

56b

55

56a

DISCOVERING THE PAST

The organisation was partly funded by the European Union, Operacional programme CULTURE, CSF III.

The display, which is presented in the last room of the Museum and forms the culmination of the tour of the exhibition, attempts to provide visitors with some answers to questions that may have arisen during their visit to the Museum, or to any archaeological museum. Questions relating to the very human, timeless need for knowledge of the past, to the methods of acquiring it, to the ways in which the material remains of the past are dated, to the fate of antiquities uncovered in modern cities, to the role of conservation, and so on. The display also describes the intellectual and technical processes that convert an archaeological find into a museum exhibit.

These subjects are presented through visual aids, particularly with the aid of modern technology. The only authentic exhibit in the room is a large fragment of a mosaic floor from an Early Christian house, found in a rescue excavation on a building plot in the Upper Town of Thessaloniki.

THE MOSAIC FLOOR adorned the triclinium of an urban villa of the 5th century. It depicts the signs of the zodiac and personifications of the months and winds (fig. 57).

Detached from its original position, the mosaic floor is surrounded and evocatively annotated by a modern visual creation, a wall-painting by the artist Dimitra Kamaraki. This calls to mind the familiar urban landscape of modern Greek towns, in which antiquities are often discovered and with which they coexist, stifled and downgraded. The display is completed by a digital retrospect of the history of museums.

57

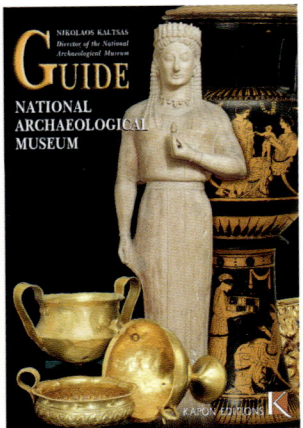

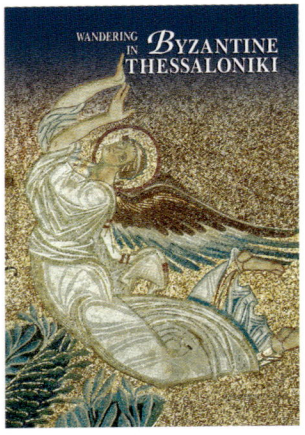

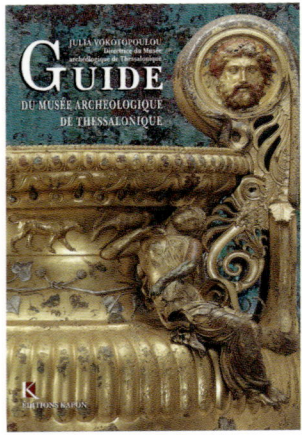

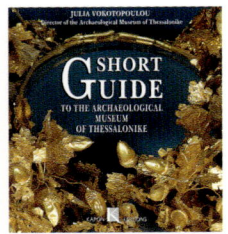

KAPON EDITIONS

Makriyanni 23-27, Athens 117 42,
Tel./Fax: (210) 9214 089, 9235 098
e-mail: kapon_ed@otenet.gr
www.kaponeditions.gr